It looked as if Grandma's overnight bag bulged with money... and it was Emily's birthday. Wow! Emily raced to open the door.

"Grandma! I knew you'd come!" Emily almost knocked her over with a bear hug. Grandma dropped her bag and several apples rolled out.

"Happy Birthday, my ten year old! I would never forget. And...I brought you a surprise."

"Apples?" Emily looked puzzled.

"No, this is for you," said Grandma, handing her a large envelope. Emily was disappointed that Grandma's bag was filled with apples and not money. As she read the gigantic card, a paper slipped out. It said "stock certificate." (Grandma was known for surprises.)

"That's your birthday present, honey.
 I bought you stock in one of my favorite companies traded on the stock market.
If we're lucky, it will grow as fast as you grow, and will pay for your college education."

Emily had never actually held a stock certificate before. Sure, she listened occasionally when her parents talked about stocks, and she knew they were valuable, like money. But she was curious. "Grandma, why is this stock certificate so good for me?"

"It means you are a shareholder and you own some of this company.
If you have 25 shares, you own 25 parts or votes," Grandma explained. "Shareholders help shape decisions made by the company's board of directors, because a company on the stock market listens to its shareholders. The more shares you own, the more votes you have."

"But...how can I be an owner when I can't even have a job?" asked Emily.

"Let's take these apples into the kitchen and I'll show you. You can help me make a pie for dinner," Grandma replied.

CERTIF
O
STO

ABC COM

76543

This certifies that
GRANDMA SMITH CUSTODIAN
EMILY SMITH
UNIF TRF MIN ACT

Cusip number

The company issuing the stock

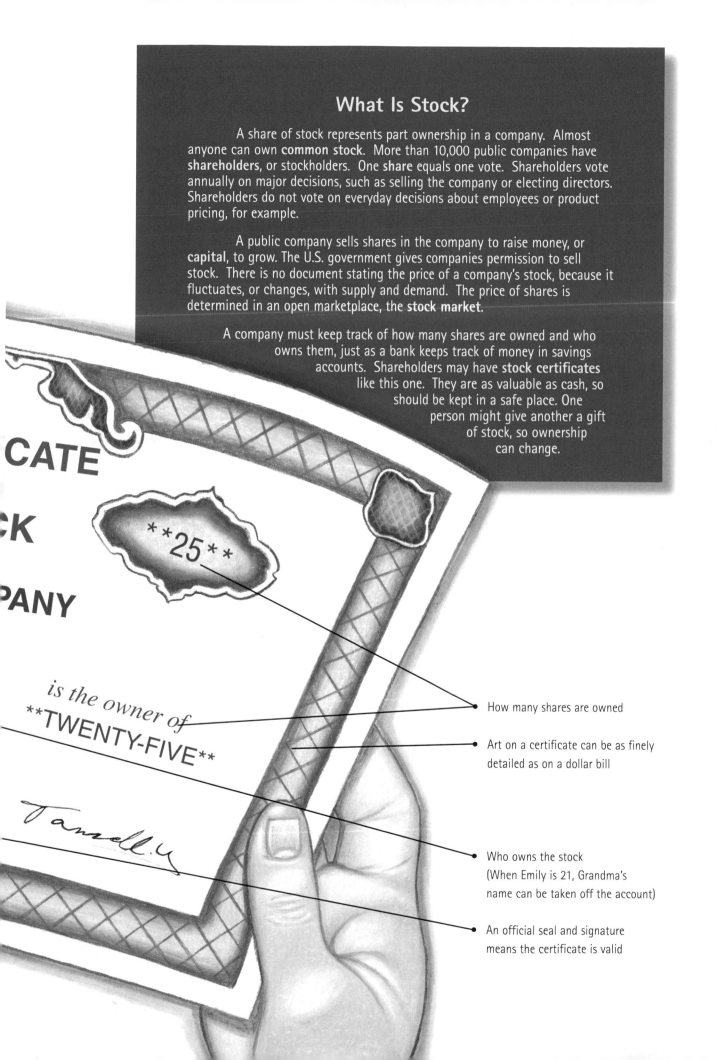

What Is Stock?

A share of stock represents part ownership in a company. Almost anyone can own **common stock**. More than 10,000 public companies have **shareholders**, or stockholders. One **share** equals one vote. Shareholders vote annually on major decisions, such as selling the company or electing directors. Shareholders do not vote on everyday decisions about employees or product pricing, for example.

A public company sells shares in the company to raise money, or **capital**, to grow. The U.S. government gives companies permission to sell stock. There is no document stating the price of a company's stock, because it fluctuates, or changes, with supply and demand. The price of shares is determined in an open marketplace, the **stock market**.

A company must keep track of how many shares are owned and who owns them, just as a bank keeps track of money in savings accounts. Shareholders may have **stock certificates** like this one. They are as valuable as cash, so should be kept in a safe place. One person might give another a gift of stock, so ownership can change.

CATE

CK

PANY

25

is the owner of
TWENTY-FIVE

How many shares are owned

Art on a certificate can be as finely detailed as on a dollar bill

Who owns the stock
(When Emily is 21, Grandma's name can be taken off the account)

An official seal and signature means the certificate is valid

Grandma peeled the apples, and Emily mixed the crust ingredients under Grandma's watchful eye.

"I'll tell Mom and Dad I have a new stock and new pie at dinner. Everyone can have a piece of pie, but I'll keep the stock all for me. It's my birthday," Emily laughed.

"Hey! Grandma! My company on the stock market could be this pie. Everyone can get a piece, but no one gets it all."

Who Are Investors?

People buy and sell stocks to make money. Stockholders don't get rich over night, and some lose money. But compared to savings accounts and many other investments, stock ownership can bring greater rewards and risks.

A stockholder can be categorized as a **speculator**, **trader**, or **long-term investor**. They can be young or old, but age often makes a difference in investment decisions.

In the spring of 1929, about 1 in 40 Americans owned stocks. Before that, investing was an activity for the rich. Today, about half of American households own stock.*

*Federal Reserve Bulletin January, 2000.

"Exactly," Grandma smiled, and she continued to cut apples into wedges. "Everyone could have different kinds of pie. That's why pies come in many flavors. No two pies are alike, and neither are two companies. Some pies are very popular, so many people want those pieces. Usually, these companies have been around a long time, and everyone knows about them. People trust they will be good investments."

Become A Great Investor

Buying a stock can be as easy as buying a car or computer. Just like any skill, however, selecting stocks takes practice. You can get help from educational books, magazines, and websites, but it takes time to learn. A good place to start is an investment club by the **National Association of Investors Corporation**.

Many individuals become great investors. Warren Buffett, who turned 70 in 2001, is probably most famous. He has amassed billions just buying stocks and American companies, making him one of the richest Americans, according to **Forbes** magazine.

Buffett lives in Omaha, Nebraska, and runs Berkshire Hathaway, a company that owns many shares of stock in other companies. He likes to drink Cherry Coke, does not drive a new car, likes numbers, and loves his work. Many ordinary people, **stock market analysts**, and the news media watch Buffett's investment decisions closely, whether they own Berkshire stock or not.

Buffett describes his philosophy as **value investing**. Essentially, he determines stock he wants and then waits for it to go on sale. He doesn't buy if he doesn't understand what the company makes or how the products are used. Once he discovers a good company, he will keep the stock as long as the economics of the company remain steady. Buffett has discovered that it makes sense to hold a good investment — "a bird in the hand is worth two in the bush," he said in Berkshire's 2001 annual report.

Of course, stockholders of Berkshire reap the benefits of Buffett's investing prowess. When Buffett took over in 1965, Berkshire stock was worth $18 per share. In 2001, one share reached a pricey $74,000. In fact, Berkshire is the highest-priced stock on the New York Stock Exchange, because the company has never declared a stock split.

"Apple pie and cherry pie are old," Emily said.

"That's right. They are tried-and-true favorites.   But when companies are newer, their stock might not be as popular yet. Some companies on the stock market are just starting and have untried products to sell. Potential stockholders have to be convinced a newer company will become a big business some day, like a popular pie," Grandma explained.

"Hmmmmm," thought Emily. "If no one wanted a certain pie flavor, you might not want to try it either. I don't think I would like a spinach pie. You might make one but if we didn't eat it, you wouldn't make another one."

"Right again," nodded Grandma. "The only problem is, we wouldn't be American if we didn't change and try new things, would we? Someone had to invent lemon pie and pumpkin pie and chocolate pie and all the other flavors everyone likes now. A smart person – or a smart company – can create something everyone will want."

Emily helped roll out the crust. "A new company is like a new pie flavor. A company with a great new idea could make lots of money and grow fast, couldn't it, Grandma?"

How Stocks Become Great

Stockholders like to see their piece of the pie grow.
- The price of a share can increase.
- A **dividend** may be paid.
Each means a company profits, so stockholders share the money.

When a company grows, it may:
- hire more employees,
- sell more goods,
- charge more money,
- expand to more locations.
Company growth in one area often means growth in another.

Rather than pay stock dividends, true **growth companies** often return profits to the company so growth continues. Stockholders must be patient to reap the best rewards. (Companies that choose to pay dividends instead are **income stocks**.)

Generally, today's successful growth companies may be tomorrow's **blue chip stocks**. For example, steel was a growth industry in the 1940s. From 1950-1973, growth stocks included Xerox, Avon, and Polaroid. During 1980-2000, many computer companies became growth stocks.

How do you find today's stocks that will grow tomorrow?
- Identify industries that sell products people want.
- Find companies with imaginative and competent management.
- Look for companies that put earnings into research and product development.

"Hopefully it will," Grandma guided Emily's small hands. "I'll give you an example. What do kids like you use all the time that wasn't around when I was your age?"

Emily thought for a moment. "TVs?"

"No, we had those...."

"How about computers and computer games?"

"Of course," Grandma replied. "Now almost everyone uses some type of computer. But a few years ago, companies that made computers or computer parts were considered untried pie flavors. Computer companies like Microsoft, Intel, Netscape, Cisco Systems and Yahoo! were new pies on the NASDAQ stock market. Investors like us were not sure if we wanted to try them because they were more risky than the our favorite pies."

"The NASDAQ? What is the NASDAQ?" asked Emily.

Spotting A Good Company

"Most people get interested in stocks when everyone else is. The time to get interested is when no one else is."

Warren Buffett

You don't need a college degree in business to discover good investments, but it does take detective skills. Remember, it's your money. Don't be shy.

Discover trends by observing what people buy and use. Find the lists of stocks published by brokers and companies such as Standard & Poor's. Does a company:
- make products that wear out fast or are used up quickly?
- provide services many people need again and again?

Good investors research companies. Use the library, news media, even store clerks to understand a company's products. Make phone calls to a company to learn more and even become friends with someone there. Read about the company's potential.

Learn to Invest

A beginning investor can turn to many sources to learn about stocks. One good way is to join or start an investment club. The National Association of Investors Corporation (NAIC) teaches new investors about the basics and will help investors form clubs. NAIC began in 1951, and continues to promote four main principles for investing:
1) **Invest** regularly, regardless of what the market is doing.
2) **Reinvest** all earnings, to let the power of compounding work.
3) **Discover growth** companies so your wealth can grow as the companies grow. No one knows where the market will go. Think long term.
4) **Diversify,** or don't put all your eggs in one basket.

If you want to learn more about NAIC visit www.better-investing.org or call 1/877-275-6242. NAIC offers a special youth membership.

Investor and Broker

Broker Places Investor's Order

What Is Wall Street?

Wall Street has been a New York City road since Dutch settlers built a wall of brush and mud along a path on the southern tip of Manhattan Island about 1609. (Indians sold the island in 1626.)

It began as a popular place to trade foreign and local currencies, make land deals, insure cargo, and buy and sell goods like furs, molasses, tobacco, spices, and gunpowder. In early 1792, merchants formed a central auction at 22 Wall Street, so brokers could buy and sell for others.

Later, these brokers met under a nearby buttonwood tree to agree to trading rules, and they decided to charge a small fee. By 1863, these brokers moved inside, forming the **New York Stock Exchange** (NYSE). A group of curbstone brokers remained outside, but later moved inside to begin the **American Stock Exchange** (AMEX).

Wall Street remains seven blocks long and is the financial hub of the world. The NYSE, AMEX, and several banks and **brokerage houses** have offices here. When today's investors refer to Wall Street, they often mean the market itself.

How Trades Happen

A stock has no set price, since **supply and demand** make it rise and fall. The buyer's representative and seller's representative must reach a price agreement. During regular hours, it often takes just a few minutes to complete a **market order**.

Trading Floor

Trade Confirmed

As she helped Emily finish the pie, Grandma explained, "The NASDAQ is just one of the stock markets, or exchanges, where an investor can buy or sell shares of a company's stock. This stock market is not just one place, but a worldwide group of organizations linked by computers and phones.

"We could also trade on many of the world's exchanges. Each one measures in its local currency. In the U.S., we can trade on the New York Stock Exchange, American Stock Exchange, NASDAQ, and several regional exchanges."

When Can You Buy and Sell?

Trades are typically executed when the stock exchanges are open. Investors can put in an order on-line anytime or whenever their brokers will take it. Some stocks can actually be traded after the market is closed. **After-hours trading** began in 1999.

How Can I Buy?

You can buy shares of stock three ways:

1) Open an account with a full-service or discount broker,

2) Open an account through an on-line brokerage, or

3) Open an account to purchase shares directly from a company.

You must be 21 years old to buy and sell securities, or stocks. If you are younger, a custodian (an adult) must open the account and will be listed as an owner until you are 21 (18 in some states). This Uniform Gifts to Minors Act (UGMA) or Uniform Transfers to Minors Act (UTMA) account is easy to start and typically has low fees.

A broker will know how to set up a UGMA or UTMA. It is similar to opening a savings account at a bank.

"When we buy or sell a stock, the order goes to one of the stock markets via a brokerage house. You can call a broker to place an order or trade electronically by computer. The brokers compete with each other for investors' orders, and they all want to sell the most pieces of the stock market pie."

"Do they sell a lot of pieces, Grandma? That would be a lot of dough." Emily giggled at her own joke.

Grandma grimaced. "Yes they do sell a lot of pieces, and they hope everyone makes a lot of dough. Investors buy and sell millions of shares every day through the U.S. stock exchanges. The busiest and fastest growing stock market in the world is the NASDAQ." Grandma popped the pie into the oven.

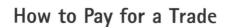

How to Pay for a Trade

An investor can place an order several ways. The most common is a market order.

When a stock is bought, an investor has three days to pay for it. (This is T+3 – trade date plus three). It was seven days. Since trades now happen more quickly, it may soon be one day. Investors usually keep ample money in their accounts, and sales are automatically deducted. If you don't pay, the brokerage can sell the stock and charge you.

When you buy a stock, you can get a certificate mailed to you. When you sell, the certificate is returned. Or, most investors have a broker hold the certificates in their accounts. This is called "held in **street name**." This makes it easier to trade.

"The NASDAQ market is not very old," Grandma continued. "It began in 1971 by linking the computer screens of its 500 market makers and automating what was known as the "over-the-counter" market. NASDAQ has been growing ever since.

"The oldest stock market is the New York Stock Exchange (NYSE), which began in 1792 by trading furs, molasses, and tobacco. Today, stock for about 2,250 companies is traded on the NYSE floor, making it the largest stock exchange in the world. The second largest exchange in the U.S. is the American Stock Exchange (AMEX). It began in 1953.

"The NYSE and AMEX traders office in New York, near where the exchanges first began long ago. The NASDAQ traders can work from computers anywhere in the world.

"The stock markets have grown quickly for another reason too, Emily."

"Why is that, Grandma?"

"Because America's companies are growing, the ones that develop cutting-edge technology, build new industries, and create new types of jobs. Investors want to be owners in companies that invent things people want and show a lot of promise to grow."

"So they can make lots of money when the company makes money?" asked Emily.

"That's right. If the new company grows and makes money, its shareholders are happy. More people want to buy the new company's stock, so they contact a broker. The company invests this new money, or capital, to try to grow even bigger. The company will hire more workers, develop more products and pay more taxes. The company's stock price goes up."

"But, what if the company makes a mistake and doesn't make money, Grandma?"

"When a company is a busy, productive place, good things can happen. More workers turn out more product which means more sales and higher profits...and a higher stock price for me."

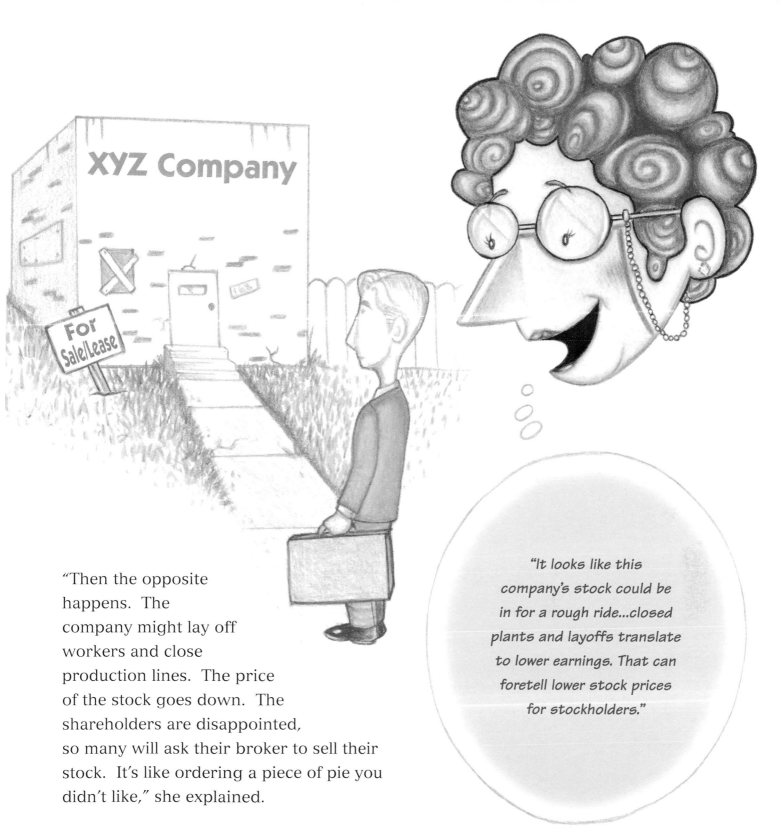

"Then the opposite happens. The company might lay off workers and close production lines. The price of the stock goes down. The shareholders are disappointed, so many will ask their broker to sell their stock. It's like ordering a piece of pie you didn't like," she explained.

"It looks like this company's stock could be in for a rough ride...closed plants and layoffs translate to lower earnings. That can foretell lower stock prices for stockholders."

"But some shareholders might hang onto the stock in hopes the company will turn around. Sometimes a company may start to do better in a couple of months. But it may take years too. A shareholder must try to think about what the future will bring and decide what to do. They also seek advice from a stockbroker."

An **Annual Report** is an information gold mine describing a company and its financial performance. It includes news, history, and product developments, plus a balance sheet and income statement. Companies must file a report each year. Investors can forecast a company's earnings' outlook and dividend prospects using these statistics to calculate the **P/E**, or **price-to-earnings ratio**, and **dividend yield**.

To find the P/E, divide the stock price by annual earnings. This is one of the oldest and most reliable ways to compare stock. A high P/E may mean a stock is too pricey or that its future is bright. Growth stocks often have higher P/Es. Don't assume a low P/E means the best buy.

Dividend yield is the amount paid to investors. To find it, divide the annual cash dividend by the stock price. Stocks with higher yields aren't always the better buys either. Companies may not pay dividends but reinvest profits to expand. This is **retained earnings.**

Buy low, sell high...

"How do you know when is the best time to sell a stock to make lots of money?" Emily said.

"That is the million-dollar question," laughed Grandma. "No one knows what is going to happen in the future. We can only guess by looking at how the company has performed in the past. You might decide to sell your stock one day, and then watch the price go up, up, up after you sell."

"But if it goes down, down, down, we'll be glad we sold, right?"

"Yes, Emily. But just as you decide to sell, someone else may decide that is a good price to buy the stock. Basically, you are trading places, just like you might trade pie flavors with the person sitting next to you at lunch if you didn't want yours.

What Is A Split?

As a company prospers and the stock climbs higher, the price may be adjusted with a **stock split** so smaller investors will still buy. This is like exchanging a $20 bill for two $10 bills.

As the stock approaches $100/share, for example, a 2-for-1 split would double the number of shares in circulation and return the price to $50. So, any stockholder who owned 20 shares at $100 each will have 40 shares at $50 each – two times as many at the new price. The value of the stockholder's investment remains the same – $2000.

Companies have different ideas about what is too high, but many will keep their price in an attractive range. Some **blue chip** stocks have split many times in their history.

"But," continued Grandma, "you might not sell all the shares you own either. You might only sell a few and hope to get a better price later. You see Emily, today each of your shares in the company is worth a certain price. If you sell, you get the price at the moment you sell. Everyday, the stock's price–or value– goes up or down, depending on how well the company is doing and news about the company."

"Many newspapers show daily stock market action. Check overall market trends or look up a company by its symbol. Companies on the New York Stock Exchange have symbols with three or fewer letters. A NASDAQ company uses four or more. You may find yesterday's closing price, high and low prices for the year, amount of dividend paid, P/E ratio, and dividend yield. Sales and recent stock splits may also be listed."

"I know," nodded Emily. "We hear the news on the radio or television or read it in the newspaper. The newspaper lists stock prices in teeny, tiny print everyday, so we can watch them." She waved a newspaper in front of her grandma.

"That's right." Grandma showed her the front page. "We get good news and bad news, don't we? We get news about the entire American economy and about other countries too. Many people in a brokerage company study how fast or slow companies are producing and how they are growing. They try to predict what is going to happen in America, based upon facts they collect and what experts say. There are reports about inflation, factory orders, unemployment,

Buying at the Best Price

Investors like to buy at the best possible price. While no magic investing formulas exist, a successful one involves **dollar cost averaging**. This means you invest a set amount of money in a stock, regardless of price. For example, you could buy $50 of XYZ stock every month. When the price is higher, you buy fewer shares, and vice versa.

Watching Markets Move

To track how stocks are doing, investors might watch a **stock price index**. No two are alike, but all show the market's direction, comparing its position at one time to another.

The most famous and longest-running index is the **Dow Jones Industrial Average**, which measures only 30 leading companies listed on the NYSE. It was invented in 1884 by Charles Henry Dow, the first editor of the **Wall Street Journal**. "The Dow" goes up or down on a day-to-day basis, and the stocks on the list don't change much.

The Standard & Poor's 500 is a benchmark that always contains exactly 500 companies which reflect the total market. The stocks are chosen for market size, liquidity, and industry weight, so members change.

The NASDAQ 100 tracks the 100 largest non-financial stocks traded for at least two years on the NASDAQ. This index is weighted by value, and membership is adjusted annually.

The Wilshire 5000 is also weighted by market value. It tracks nearly every regularly traded U.S. stock – more than 6,500.

Bulls and Bears

You may have heard about the Crash of 1929, when panic selling wouldn't stop. October 29 was the single worst day, but prices actually dropped for several weeks. The bull market of the 1920s ended with the NYSE losing half of its value.

The Crash began because large investors were manipulating stock prices to get richer. Smaller investors who were dreaming of instant wealth kept buying stock at higher and higher prices, often with life savings or borrowed money.

From November, 1929 to February, 1930, the market made a little recovery, but economic news worsened and the Great Depression ensued. Congress passed laws to regulate the economy and markets, but recovery still took 10 years. The FDIC (Federal Deposit Insurance Corporation) and banking reforms were put in place to insure against another devastating crash. The U.S. government formed the Securities and Exchange Commission to police Wall Street actions.

It wasn't until the 1960s that stock market investments became popular again. Then came another bear market in 1973-74. Americans saw another major crash on October 19, 1987, when institutional traders tried to sell large blocks of stocks. The Dow lost 507 points as computerized selling orders automatically triggered. The NYSE then made new rules to regulate large-scale selling and computerized trading.

In 2001, the NYSE traded stocks in about 1,600 companies, making it the largest exchange in the world. Twenty-two trading posts track all buy/sell offers, and more than a billion shares can change hands in one day. While ticker tape machines were once used to track prices, computers now register hundreds of orders simultaneously. A seat on the NYSE is not an actual place to sit, but a membership entitling a brokerage company to trade.

The AMEX is the second largest exchange in the U.S., listing about 800 companies. It also operates with a trading floor.

By volume, the NASDAQ ranks as the second largest exchange in the world and is the first electronic stock market. NASDAQ is the fastest growing market in the U.S., and trades the stock of more than 5,100 companies. Instead of the traditional trading floor, more than 500 dealers – known as market makers – make trades via computer.

crop prices, retail sales, and many other things. Investors and brokers like to listen to these reports, so they can decide if we're in a bull market or a bear market."

"A bull or bear market, Grandma?"

"That's how economists describe good and poor time periods of the stock market, Emily. A bull market means stock prices are charging up, just like an excited bull thrusts up with his horns. That means companies are doing well, so they share the profits with their investors or shareholders. But a bear market describes just the opposite, because bears beat down with their claws. Investors get nervous in a bear market if some companies aren't doing as well as everyone thinks they should. Stock prices may drop a lot when many investors sell a lot of shares."

Bulls Charge Up, Bears Pull Down

A true bear market occurs when a market decline of 20 percent or more stretches over a number of months or years. Down markets got this name because a bear knocks down its victims and will attack with a downward stroke of its claws. Major bear markets occurred in 1929, 1974, and 2001.

Because a bull attacks by aggressively thrusting up with its horns, a bull market indicates stocks are climbing steadily up over an extended time. America's first bull market happened in 1792, and the latest began in 1990.

Emily was a little confused, because she was thinking she should keep her stock certificate for a long time, maybe until she needed money for college. "Should we sell if the stock price drops tomorrow?"

"No, honey. The bears come and go. You just have to be patient and not panic, just because a stock price fluctuates. In fact, some stocks always jump up during certain times and drop lower during other seasons or market cycles. They are called cyclical stocks, because their prices go up and down in the same pattern, time after time. You have to watch the cyclical stock prices carefully, so you don't panic and sell when the price dips temporarily."

The Magic of Compounding

Time is a great friend to patient and steady investors who want to build big nesteggs. In fact, many ordinary people who save and invest regularly can retire as millionaires. This chart shows how investing just $20 a month can add up—that's only $5 a week (or about a can of pop a day). If you keep adding the same amount and let the interest or earnings accumulate too, your investment compounds more quickly. In the past, the stock market has returned an average of about 10% a year. However, past performance is no guarantee of future earnings.

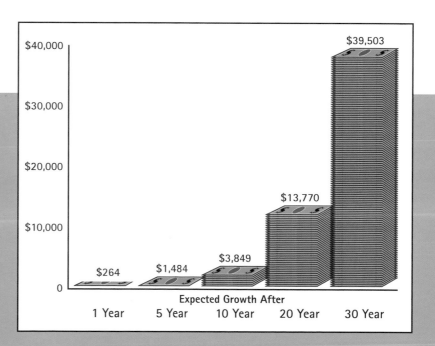

*This chart is based on a 7.5% return.

To get an idea how fast any one investment can grow, use the rule of 72. Simply divide 72 by the annual return. Your answer is the number of years it takes to double your original investment. For example, a stock returning 9 percent allows your money to double in 8 years.

"Hey, I know!" giggled Emily. "Pumpkin pie would be cyclical, because we eat it mostly at Thanksgiving. Can we make one? It's my favorite, along with stock market pie, of course."

Grandma opened the oven door and that unmistakable apple-and-cinnamon aroma filled the kitchen. "Sure we can. Those are my favorites too. But let's have a piece of this hot apple pie right now. Happy birthday, Emily!"

Did you know?

- Ticker tape parades were a Wall Street tradition of honoring heroes.

- The market does not advance in a straight line, but has trended upward since it began.

- The Securities and Exchange Commission was established in 1934 to regulate the market.

- The Dow Jones Industrial Average broke 2,000 for the first time in early 1987.

- In the short term, the price of a stock is influenced by market direction, news or events, and factors affecting the industry.

- About 80% of American businesses are owned by one person, who usually doesn't sell stock.

- A company can issue as many shares as it wants. The government gives permission.

- Two types of investors exist-institutional and individual. An institution might buy or sell 500,000 shares of stock in one transaction.

- Insider trading-where stock is bought and sold before company news is published-is illegal.

- Americans changed the way they thought about money in the 1920s when investing became easier to do.

- In 1927-1929, about 3 million Americans owned stock (1 in 40); about 500,000 used margin accounts; speculators comprised less than half of 1% of the population.

- On Black Thursday, October 24, 1929, 13 million shares of stock were sold at the NYSE. On Tuesday, October 29, 1929, 16 million shares traded. The NYSE's usual busy day was 2 or 3 million shares.

- The first bull market was 1792.

About the author

J.M. Seymour has been a professional writer, author, and investor for more than a quarter of a century. Seymour's children's books help educate both parents and children on timely topics.

The author joined an NAIC investment club in 1987, and later served as club president. An Iowa State University alum, the author and spouse presently reside near Des Moines, IA. Together, they have helped their children learn the basics of saving and investing.

About the illustrator

Artist Marcos Ramirez lives in Des Moines, Iowa, and has been a professional boxer since August, 2000. This is his second children's book.